Cute

FLOWERS

GRAYSCALE COLORING BOOKS

VOLUME 4.

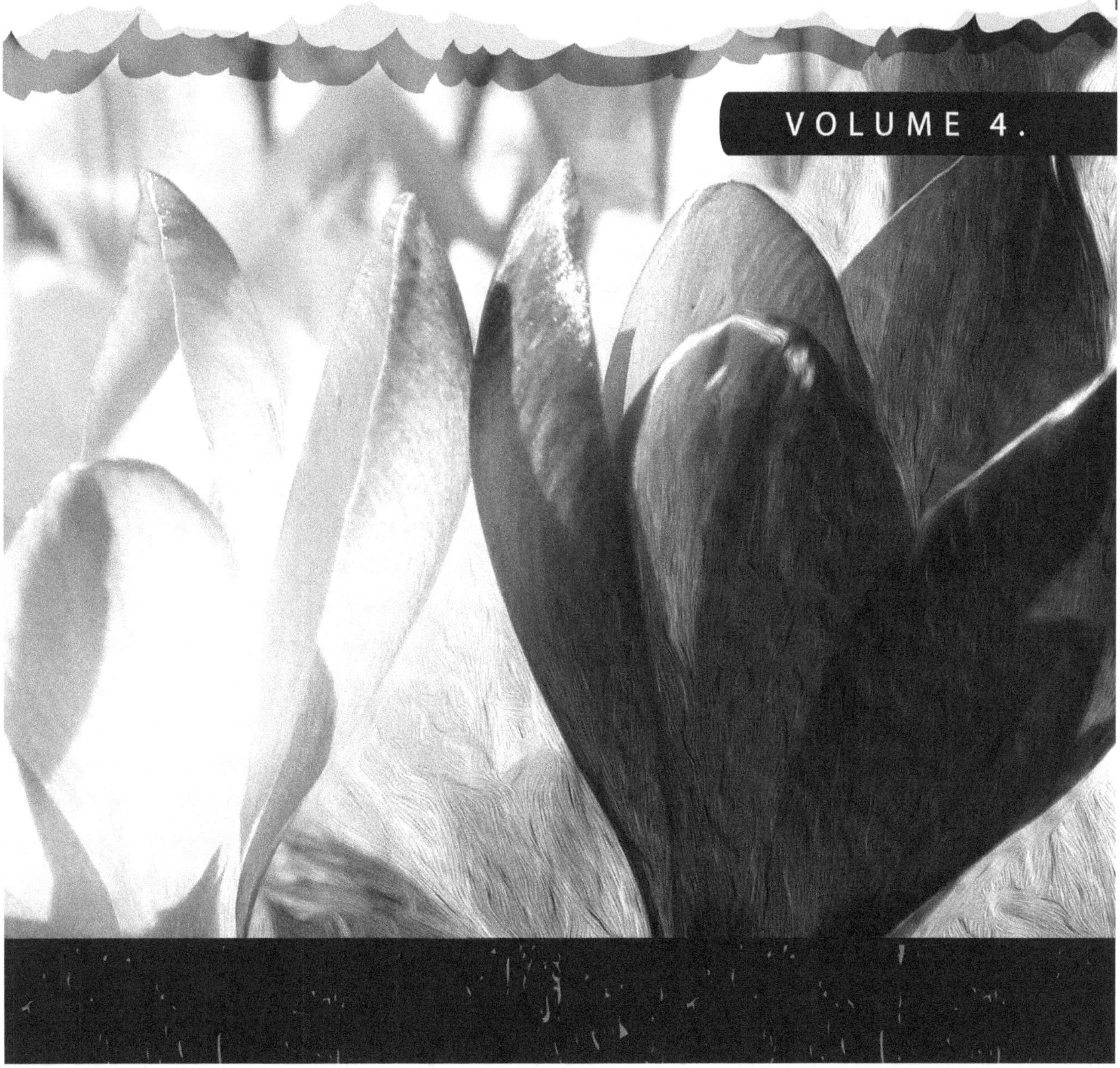

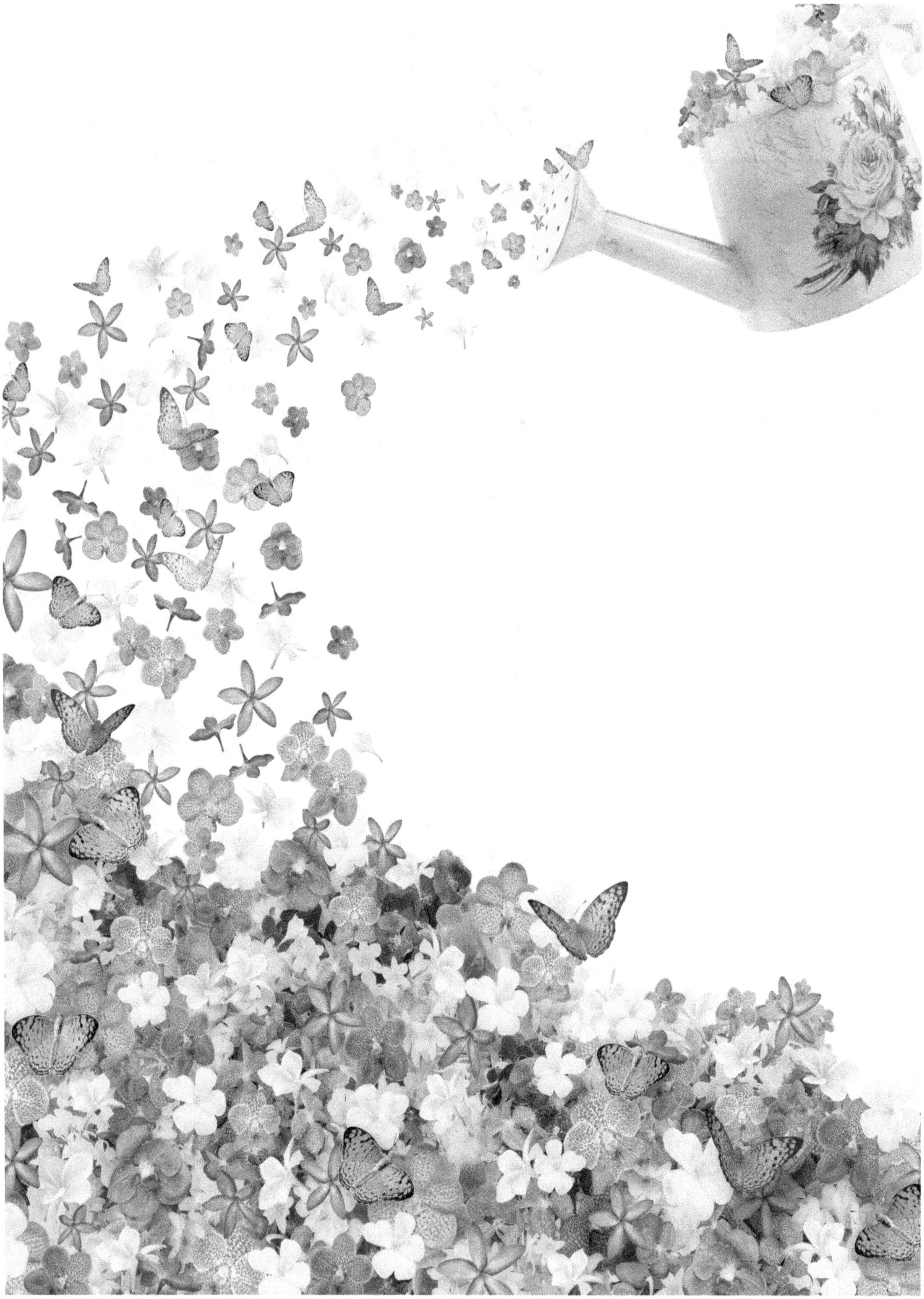

COLOR TEST PAGE

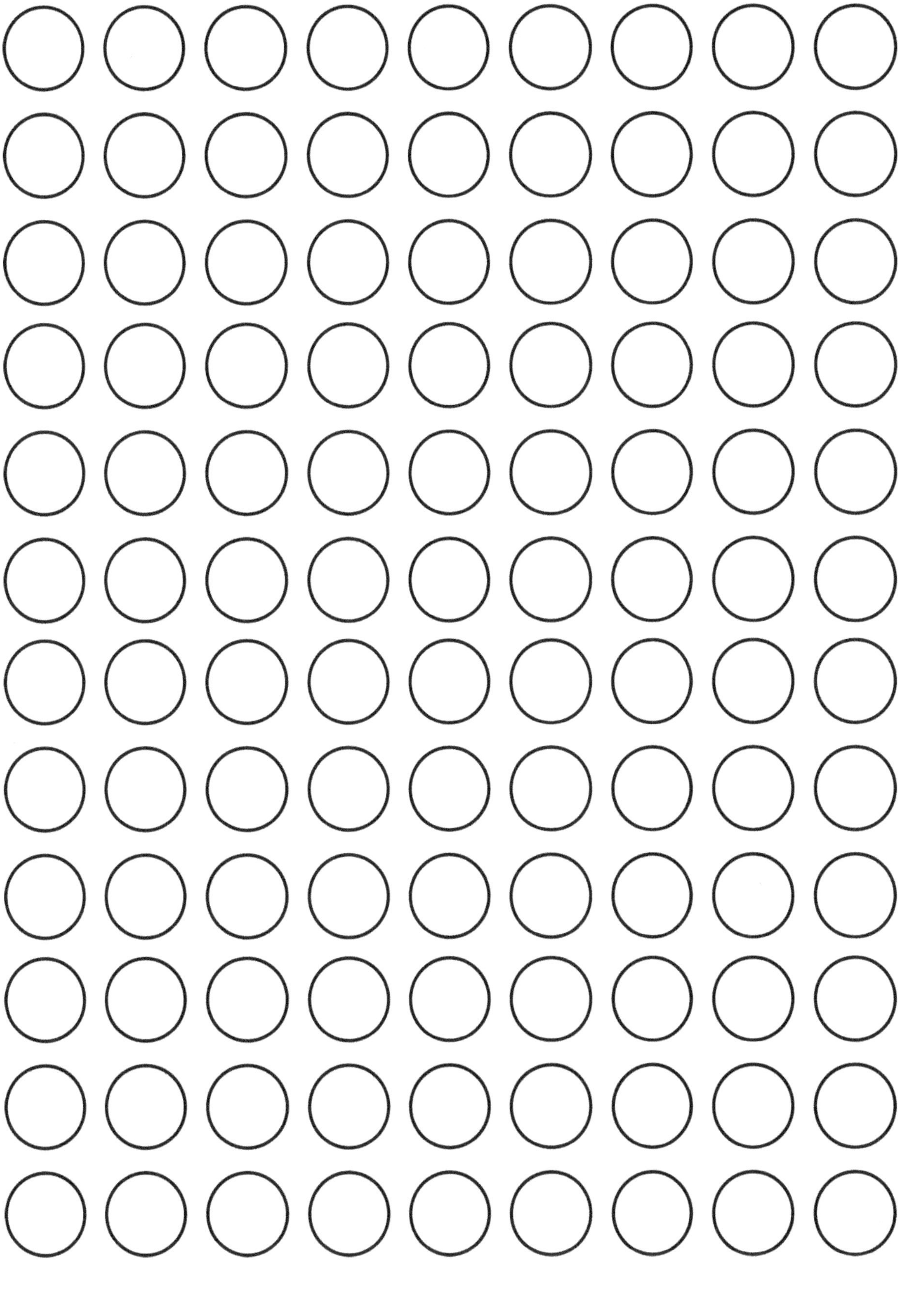

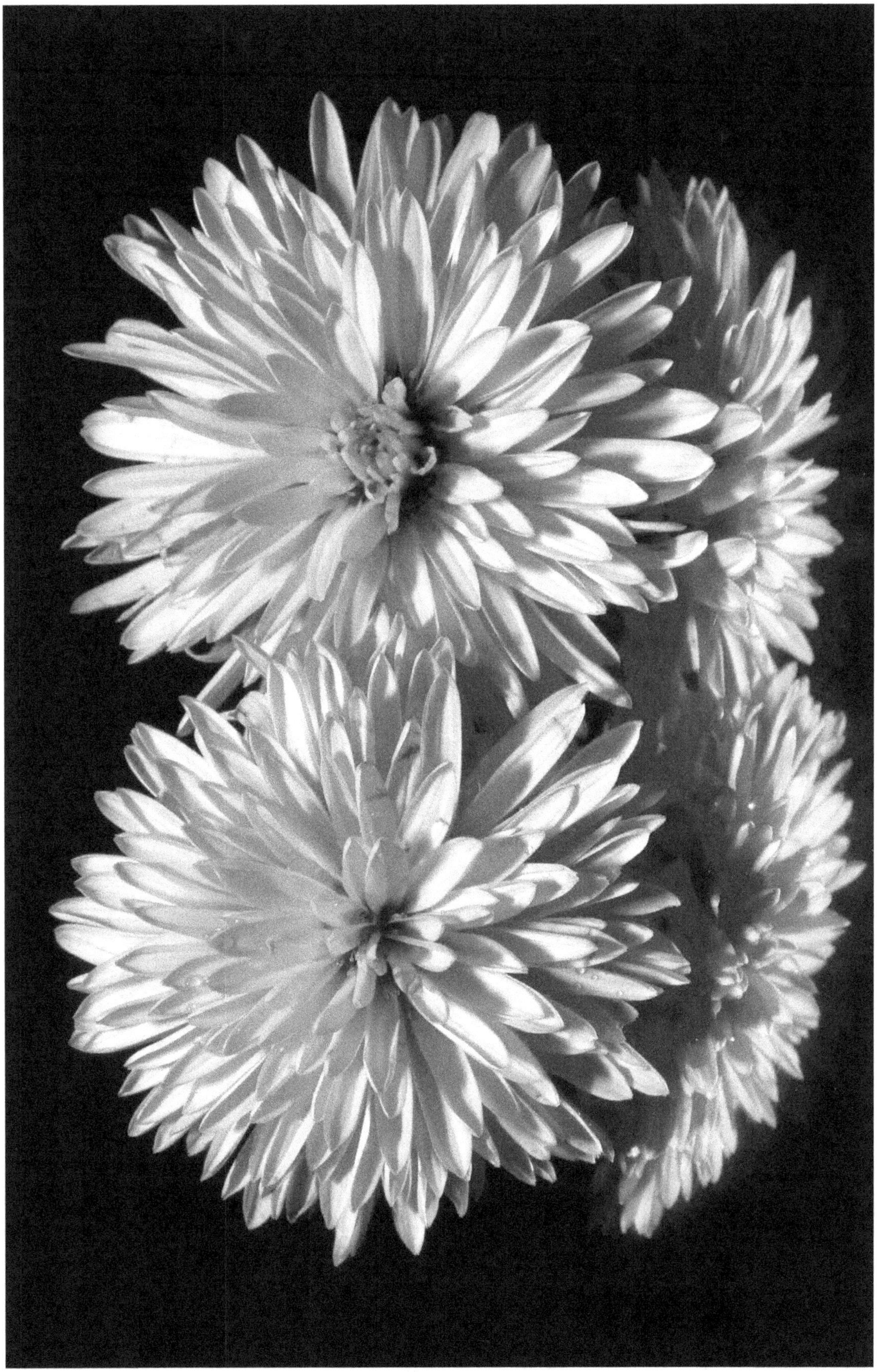

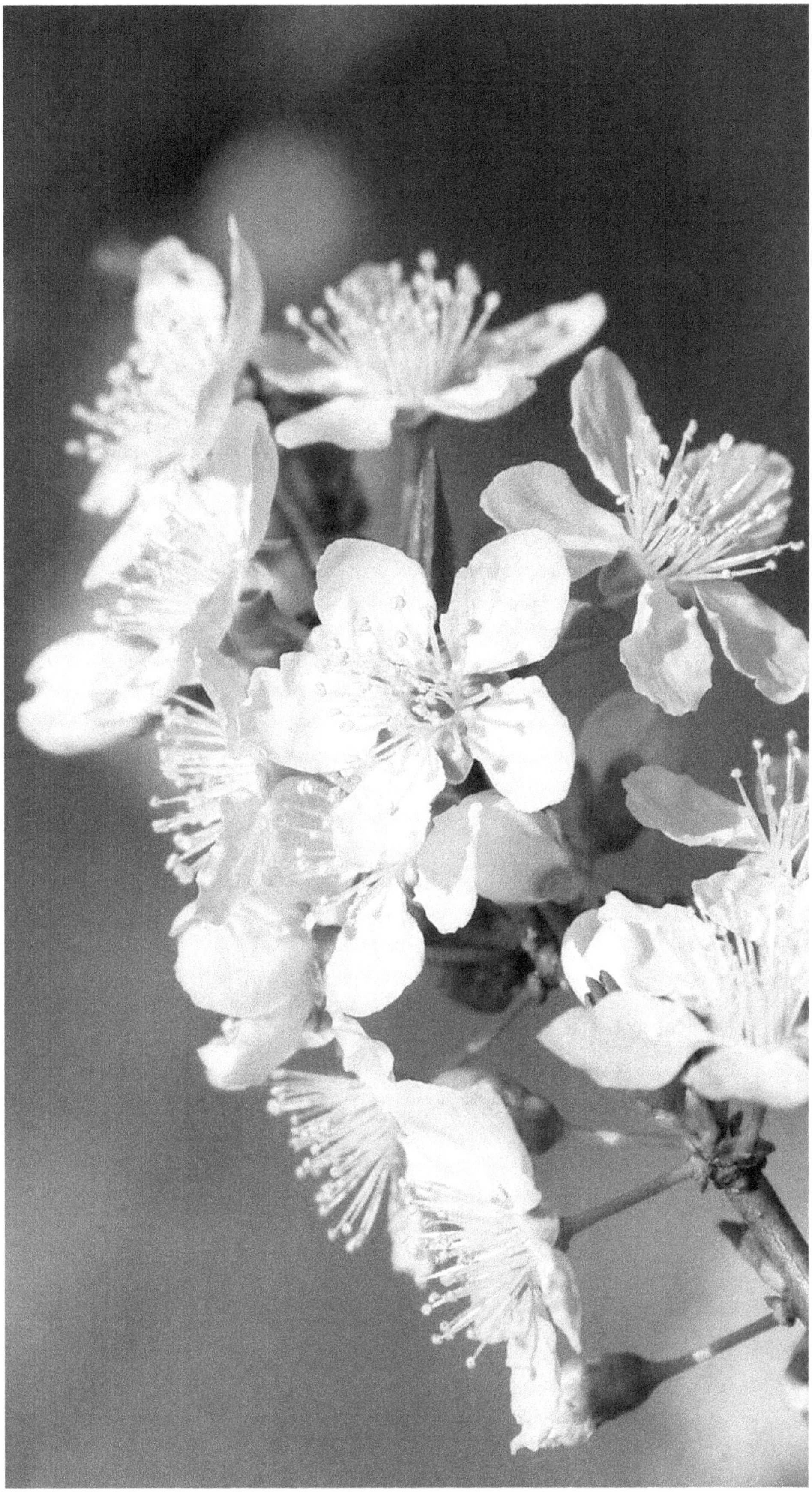

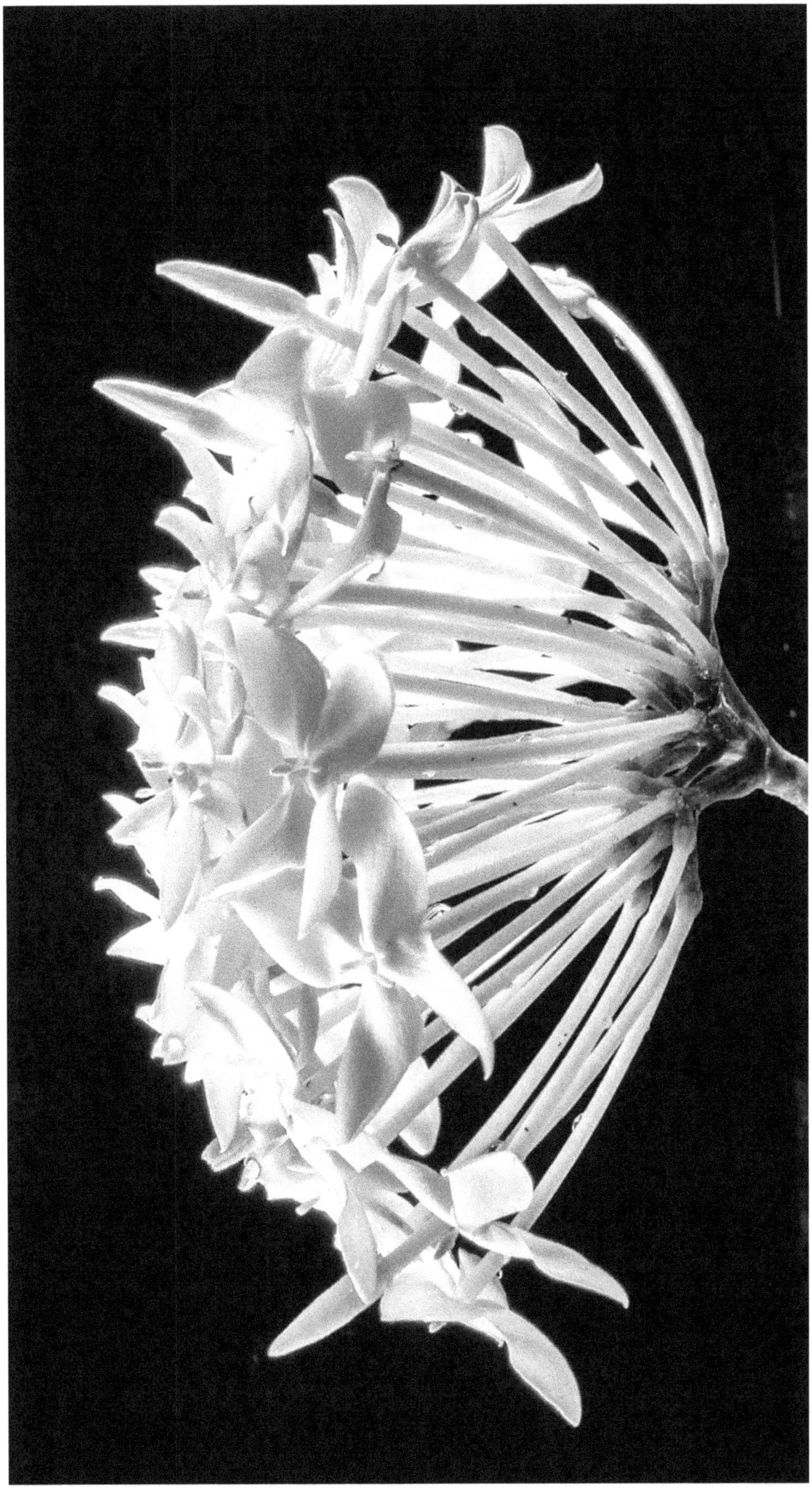

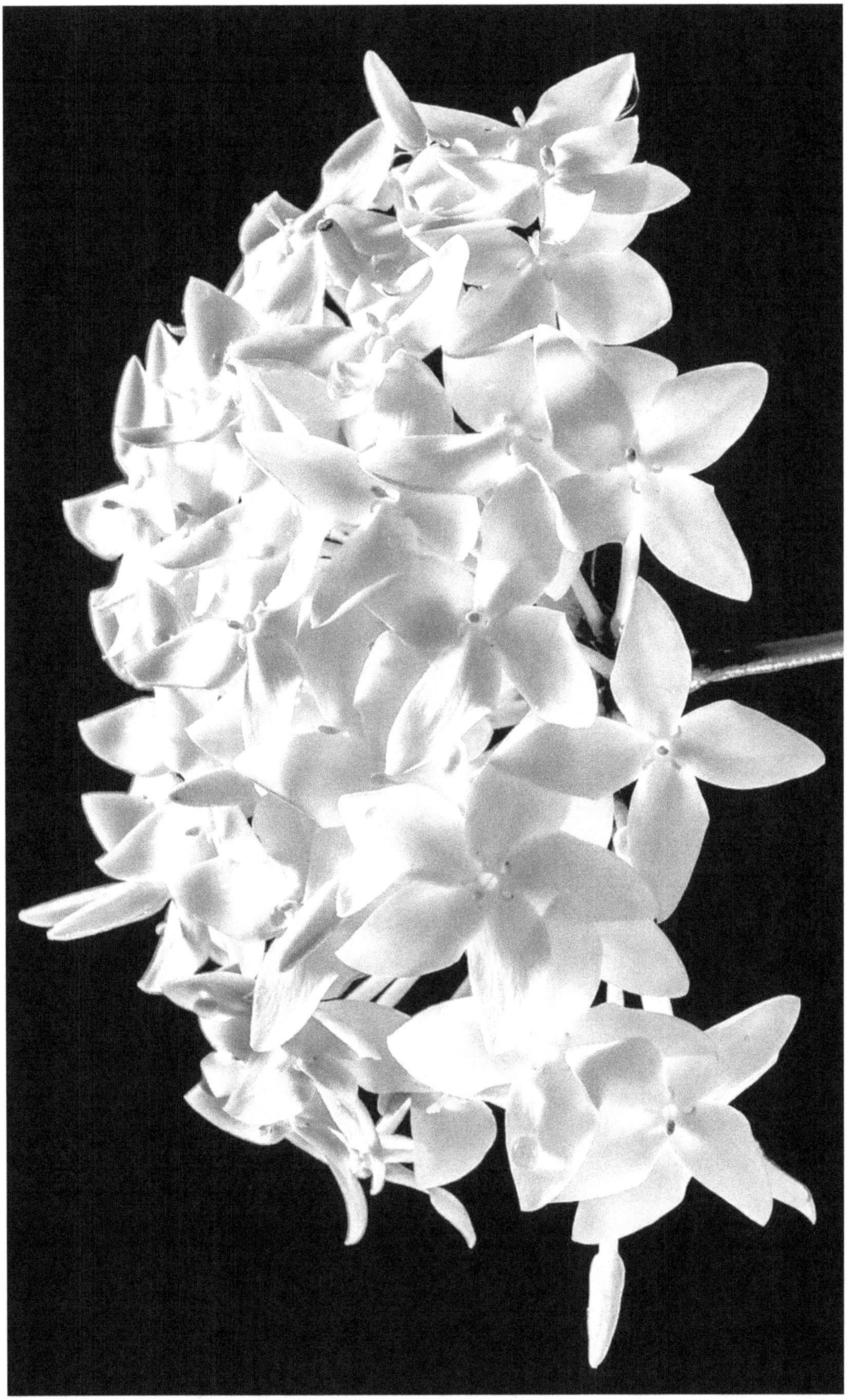

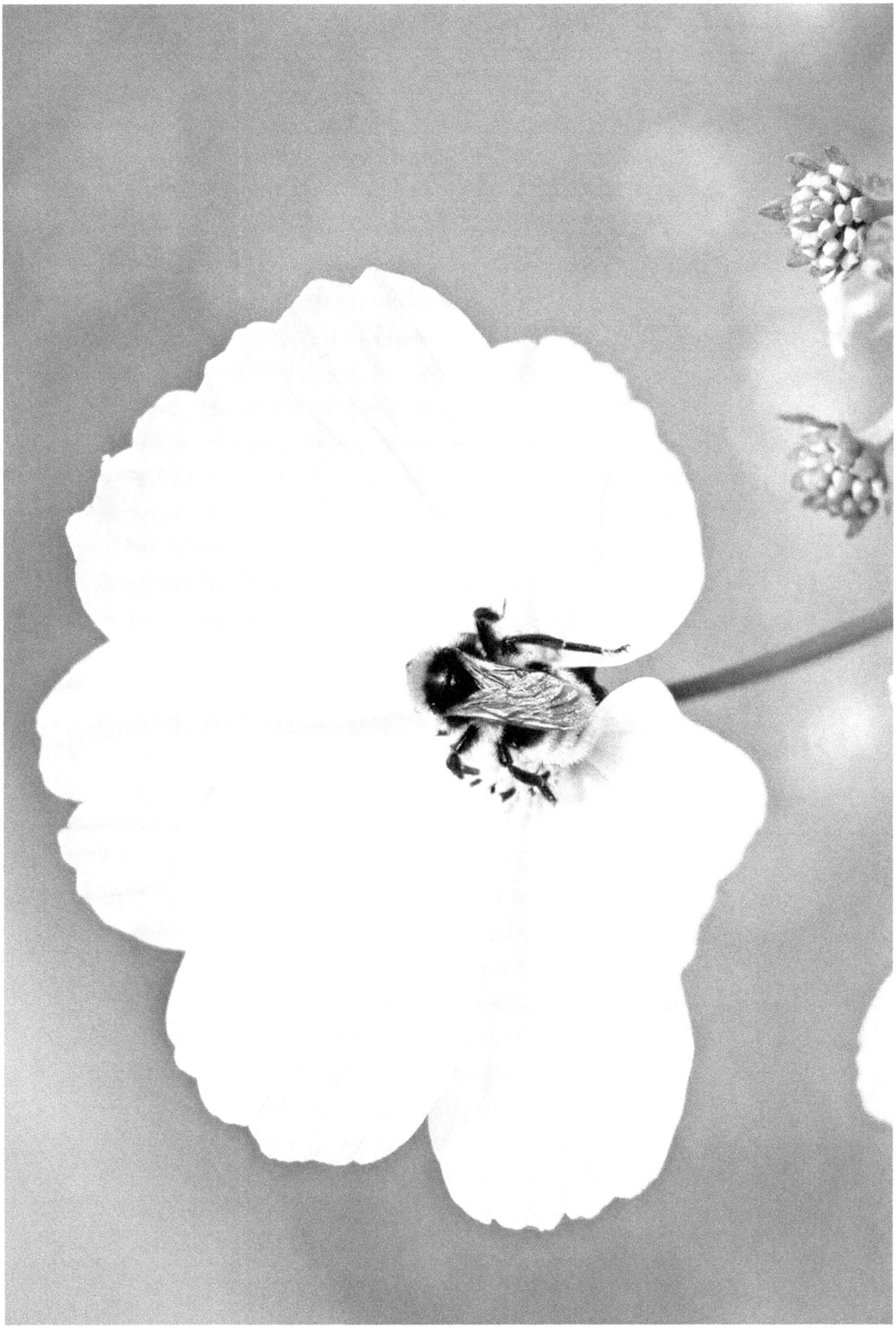

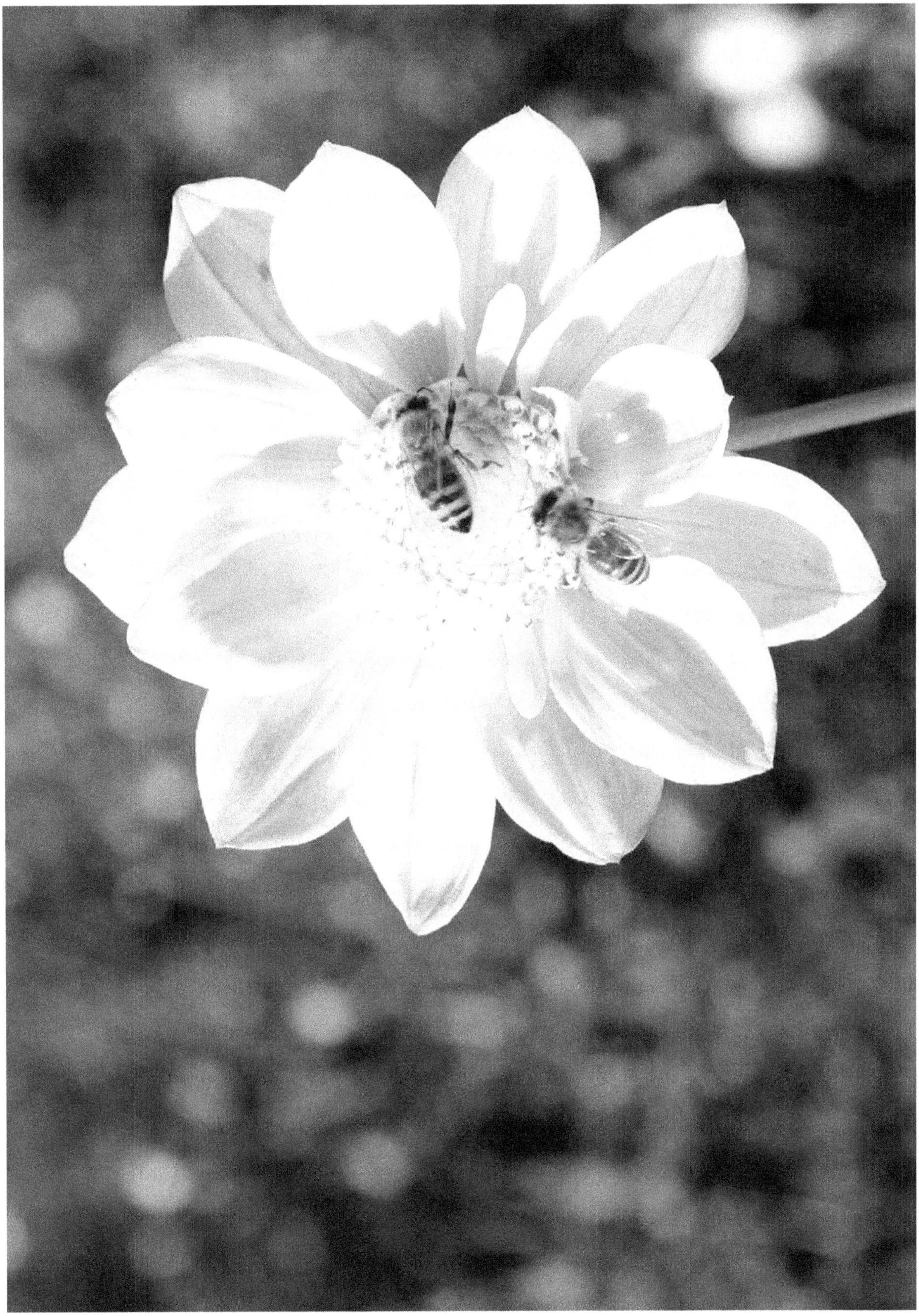

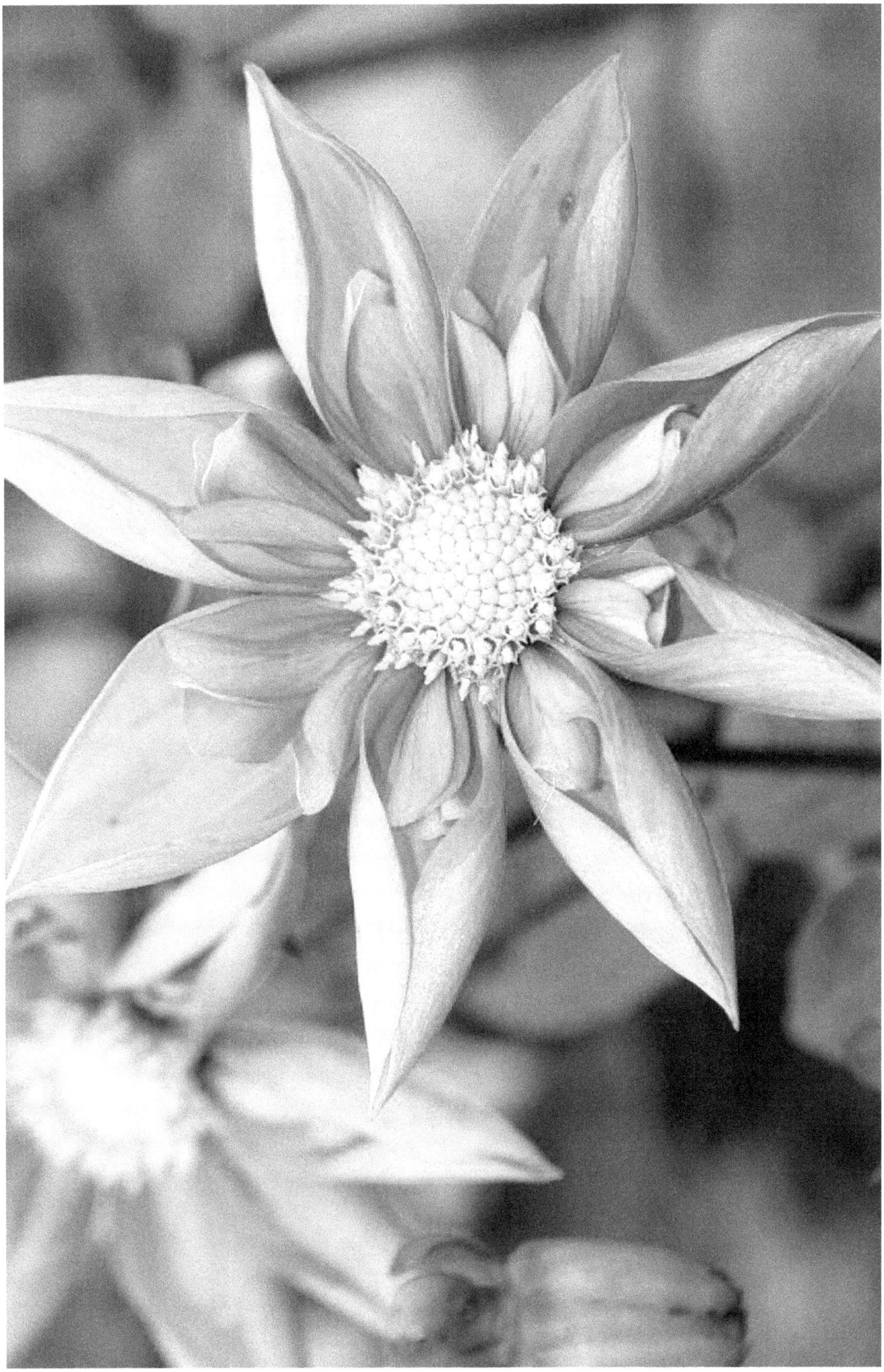

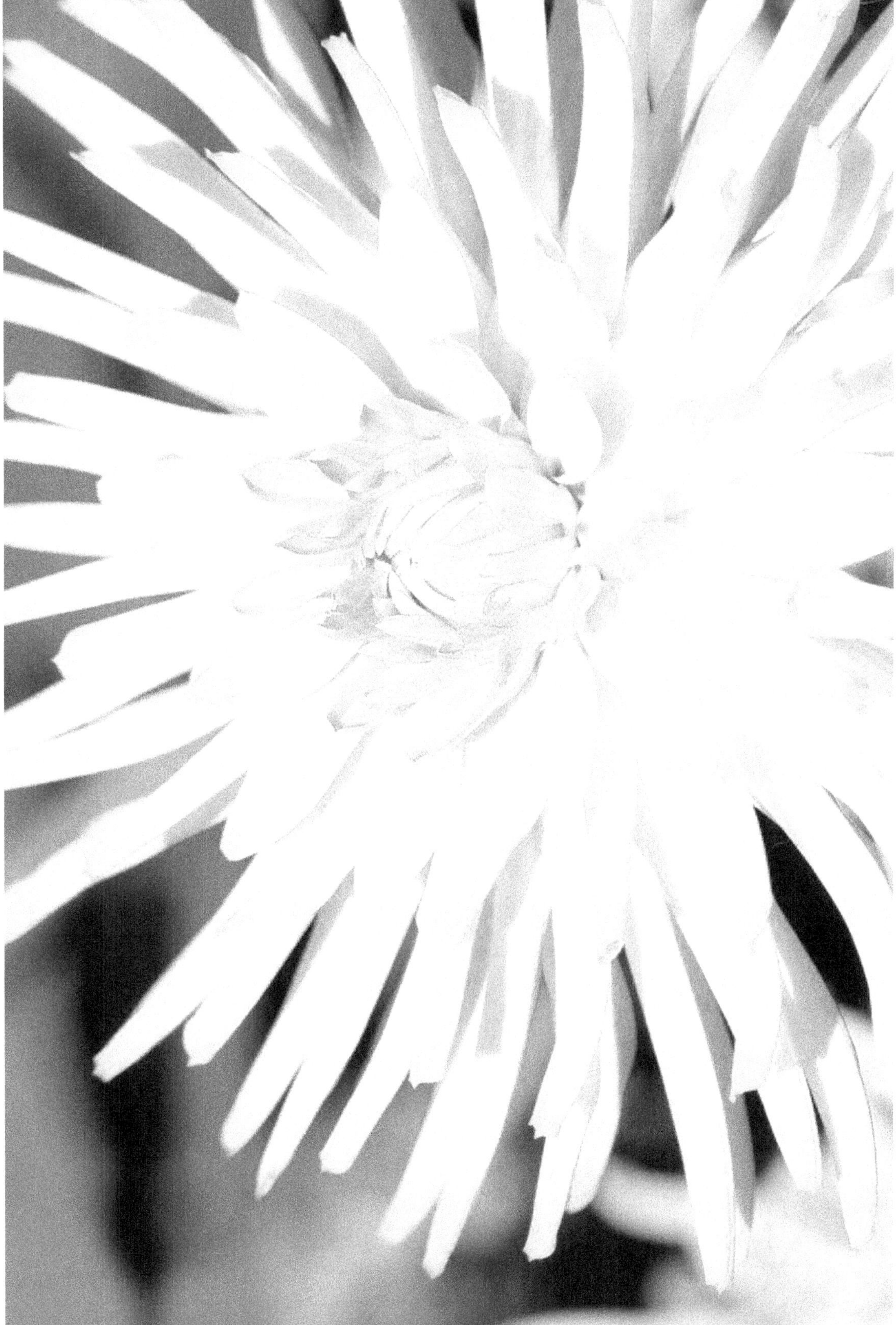

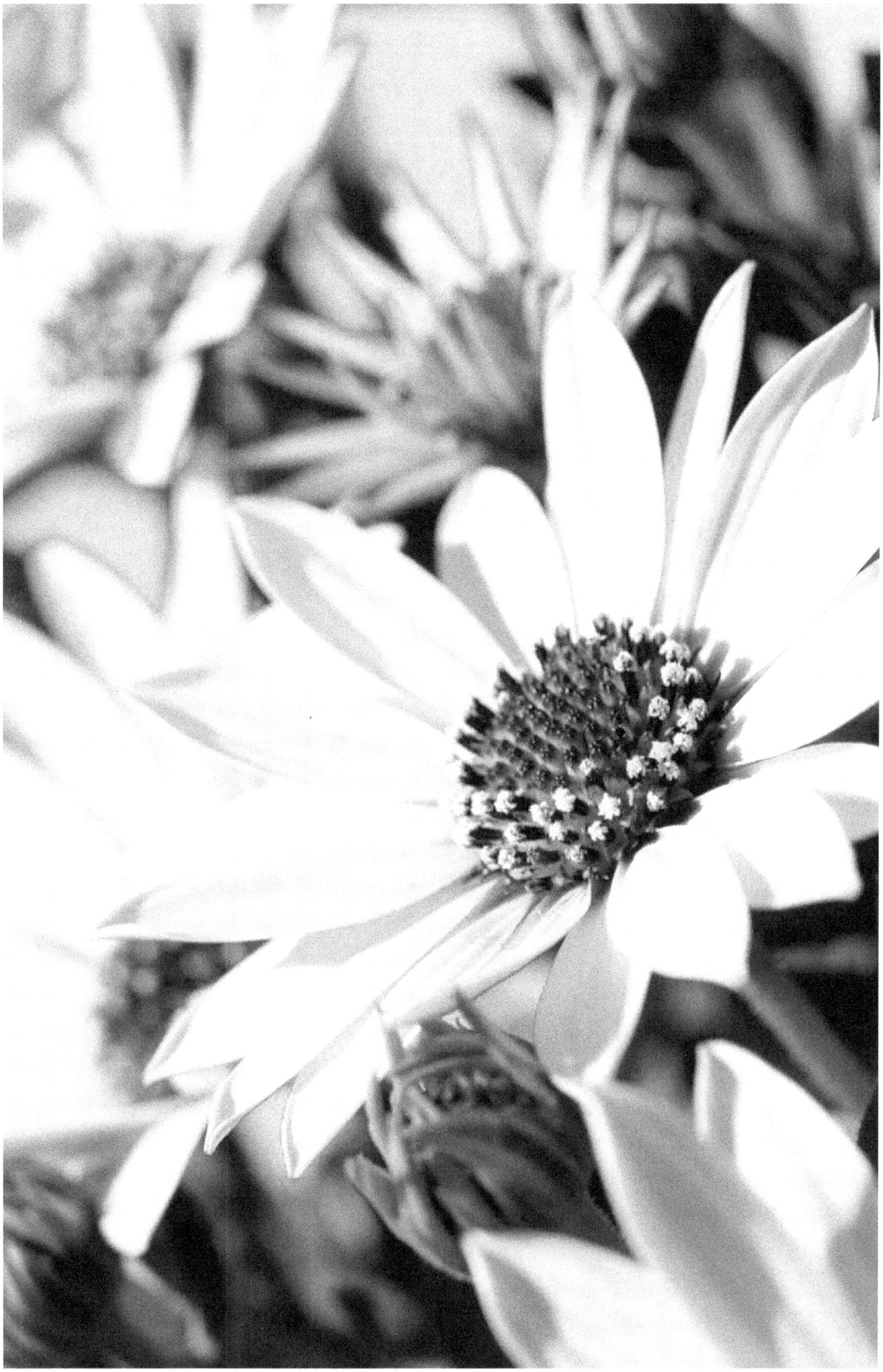

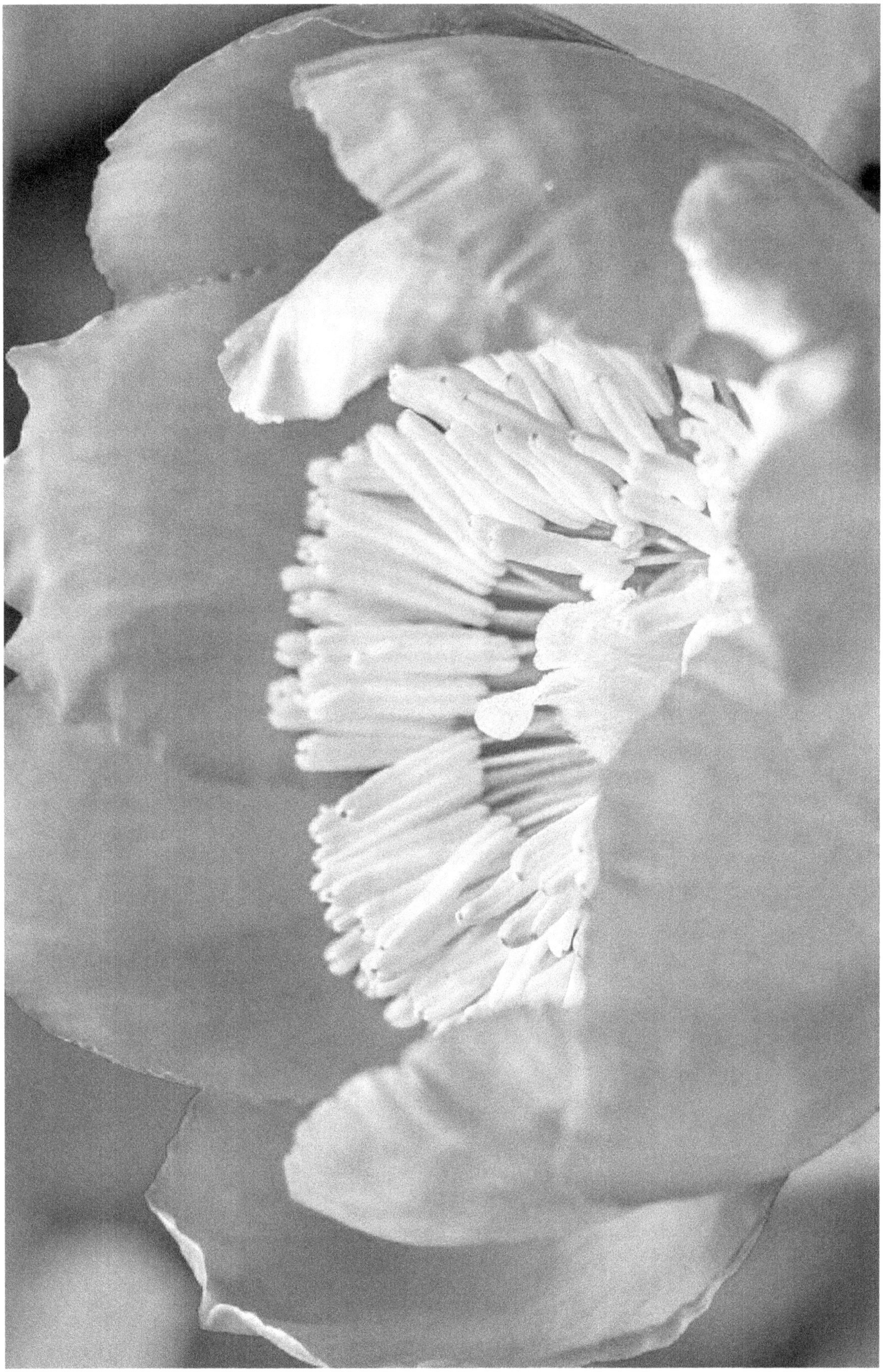

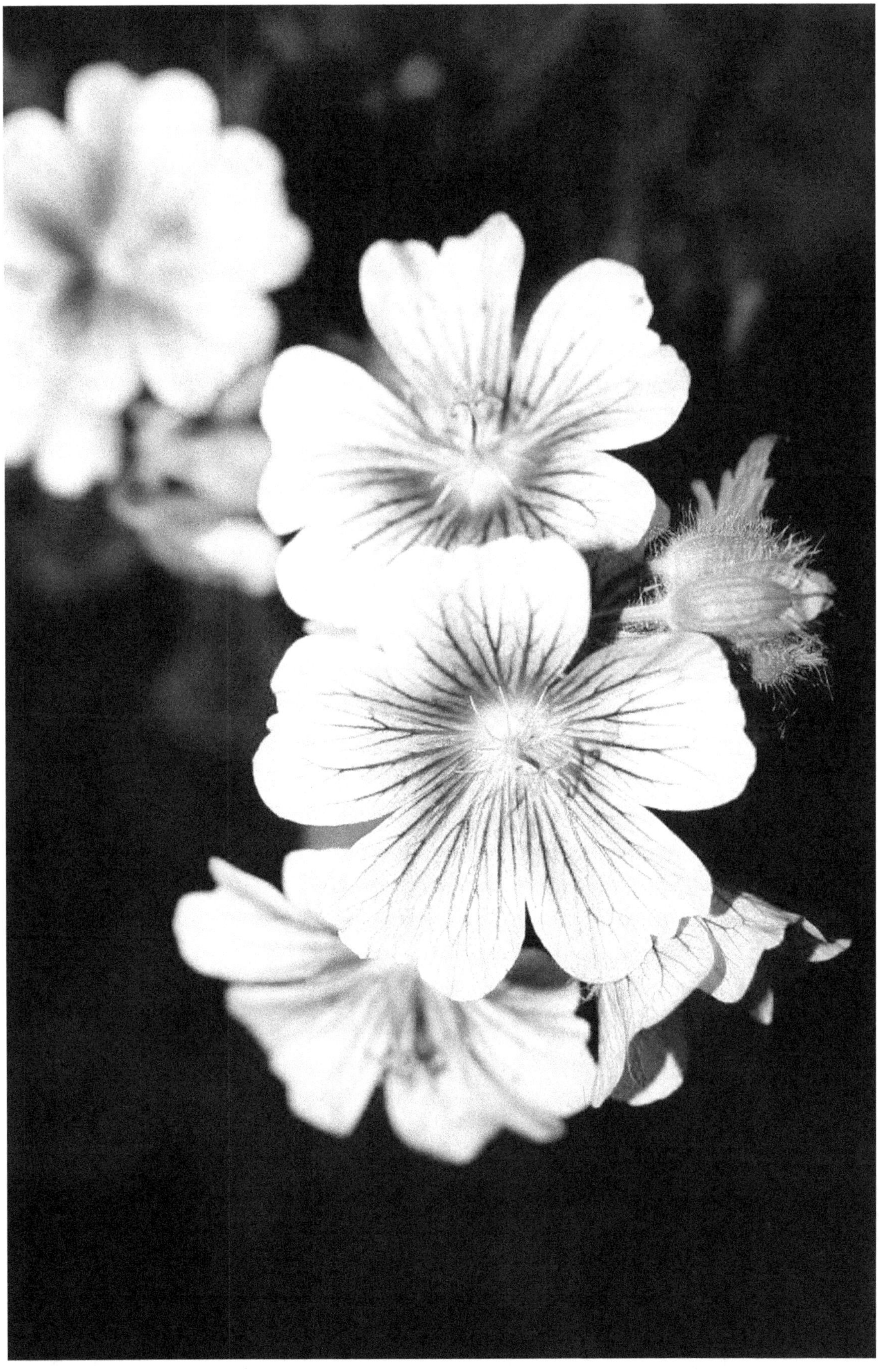

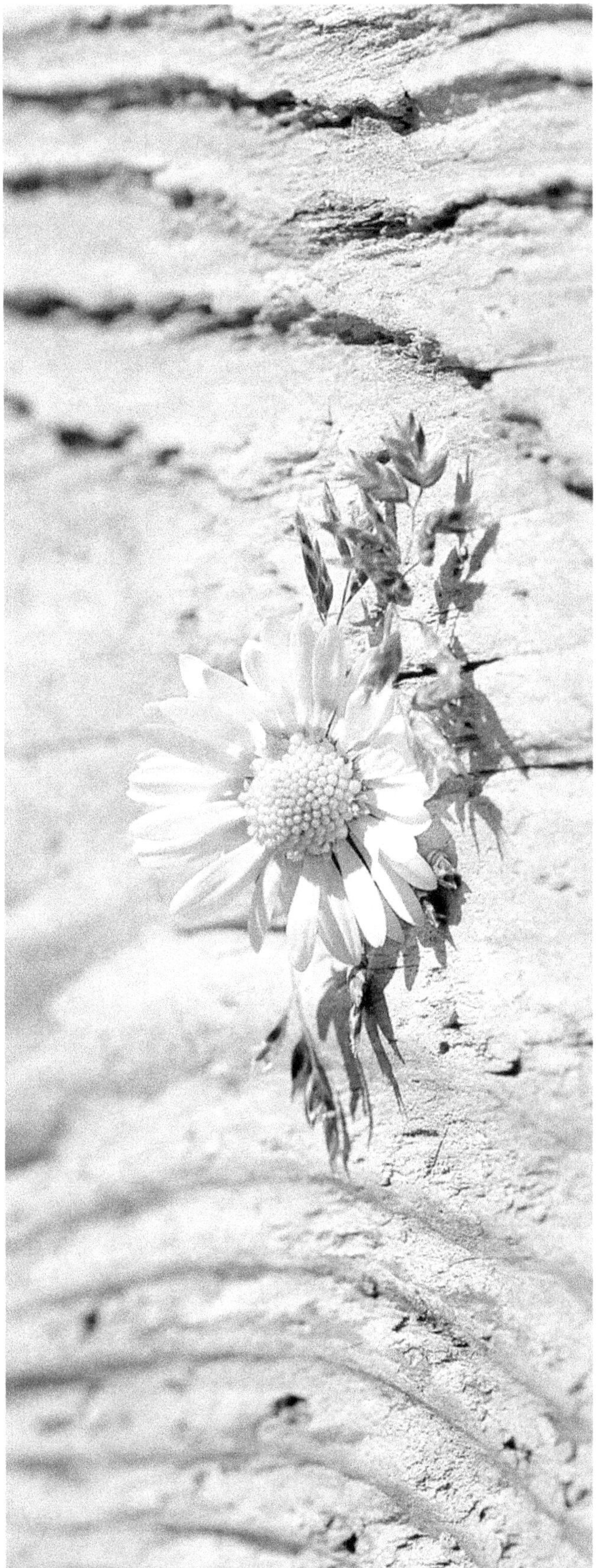

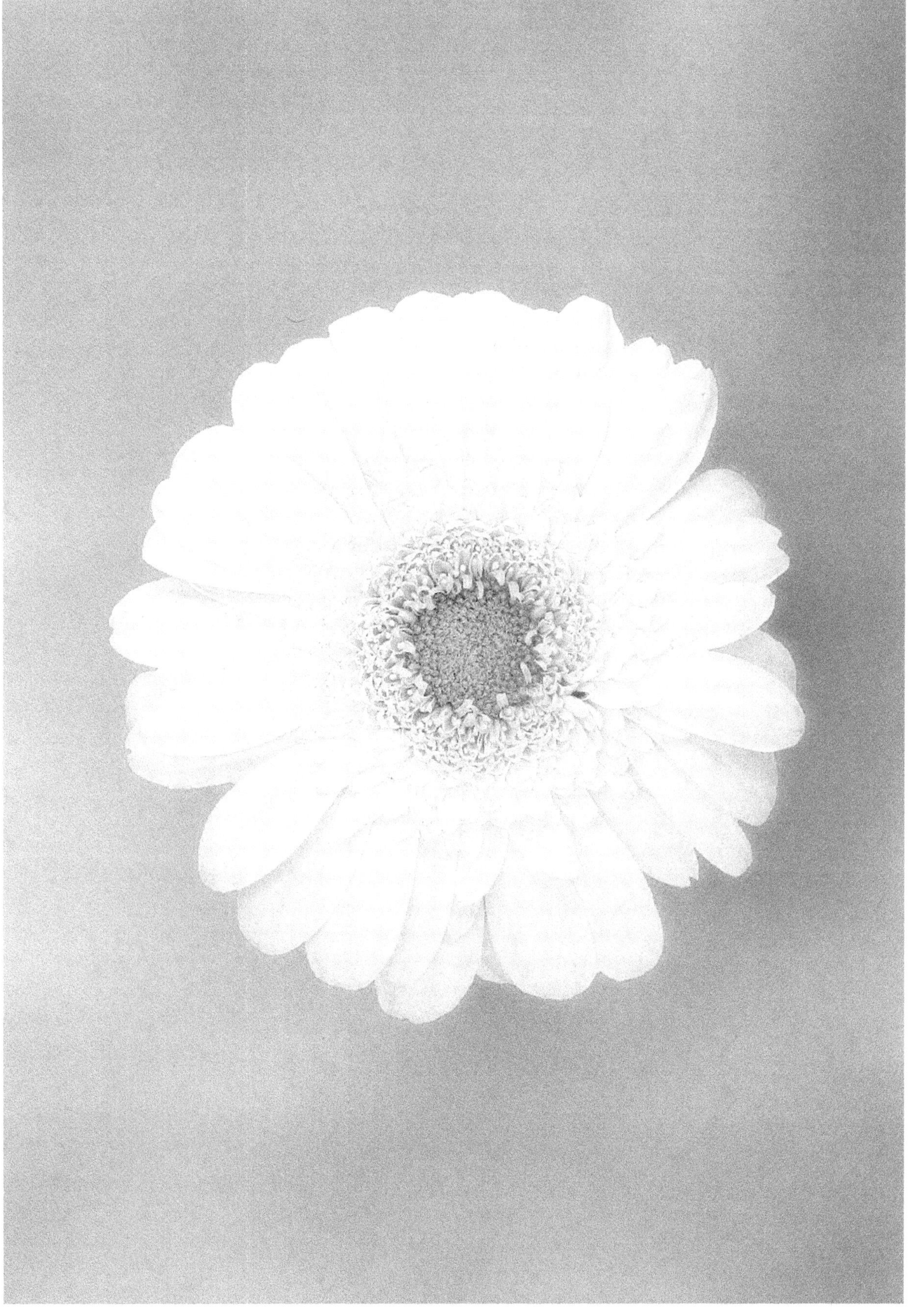

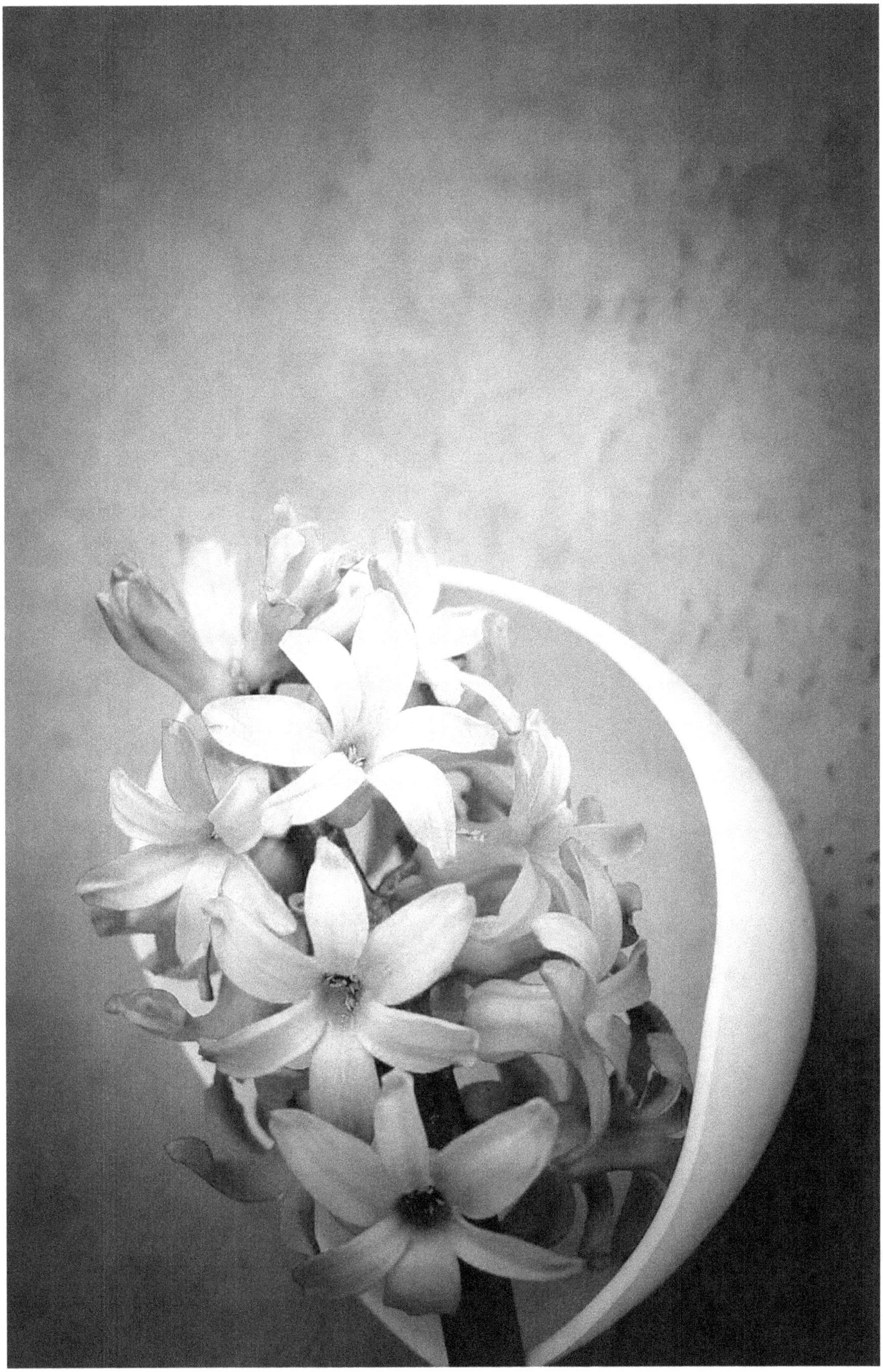

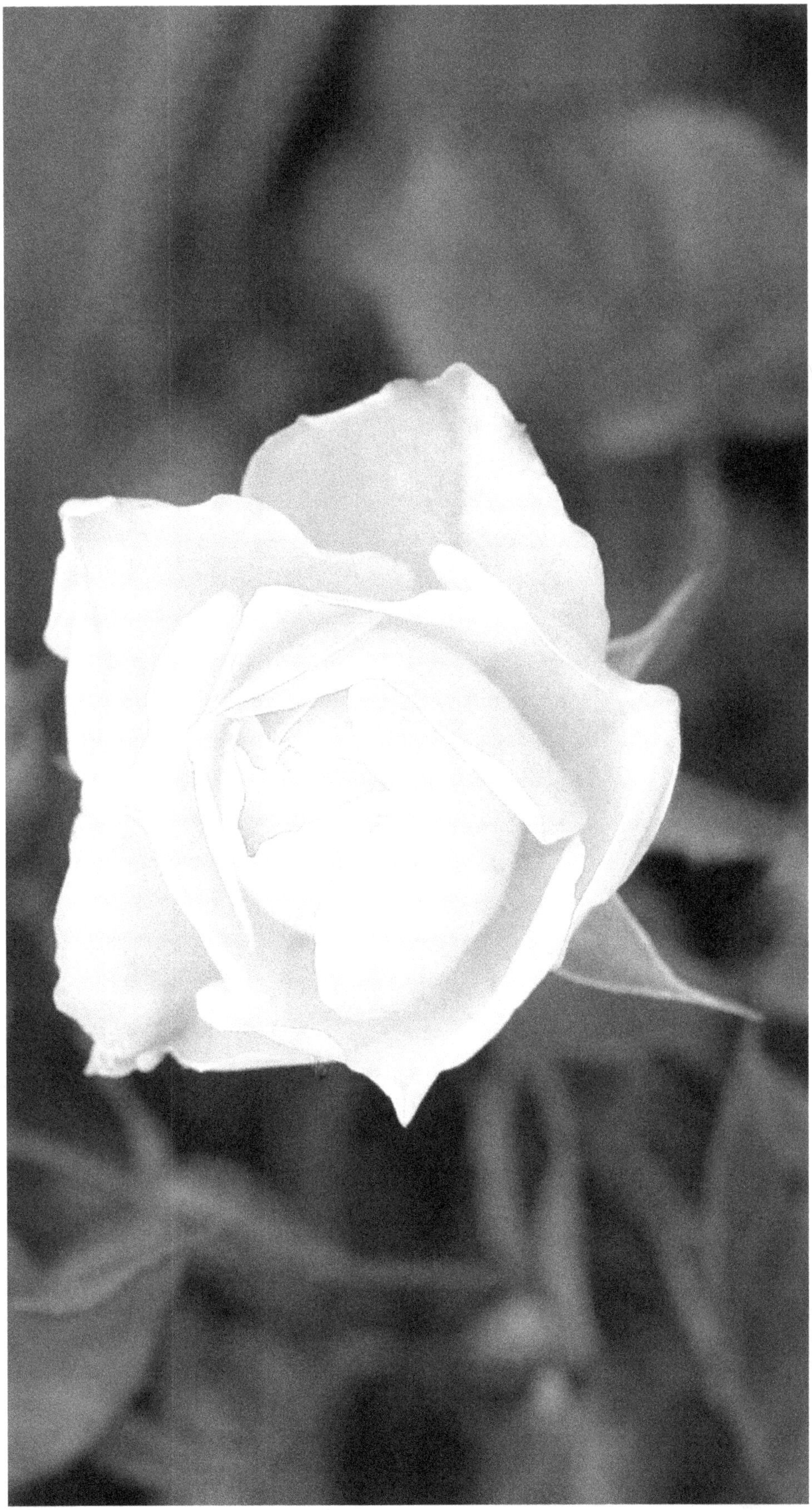

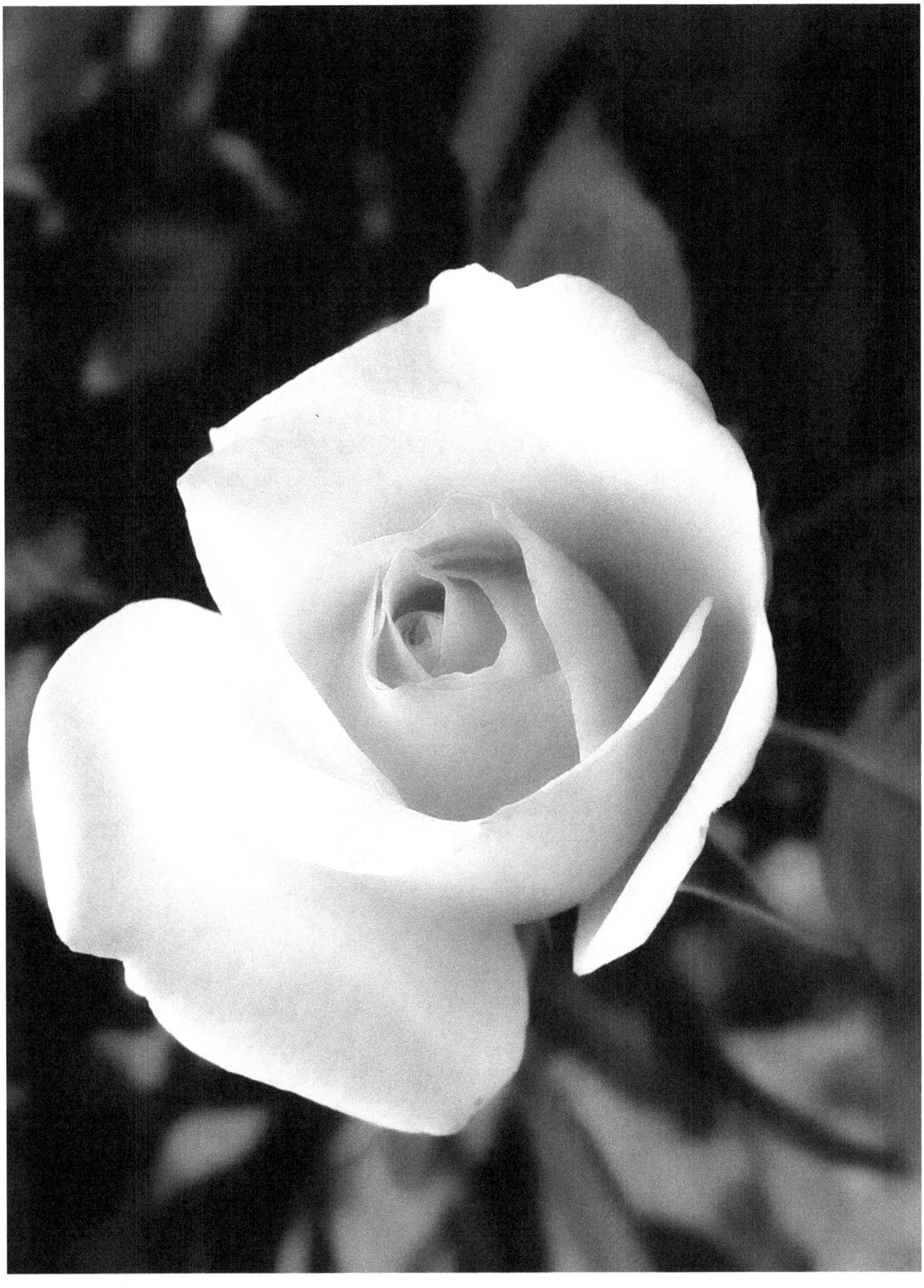

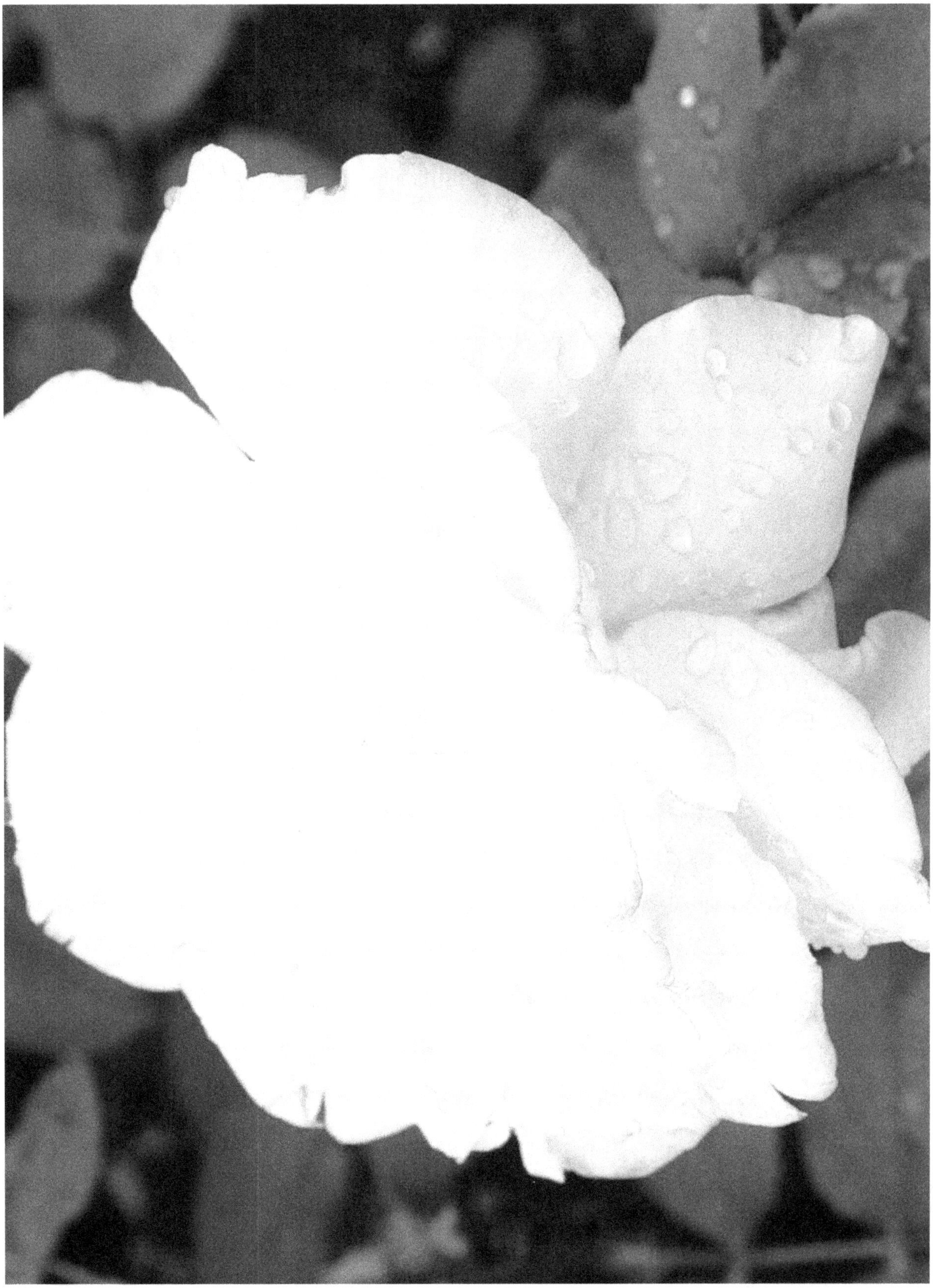

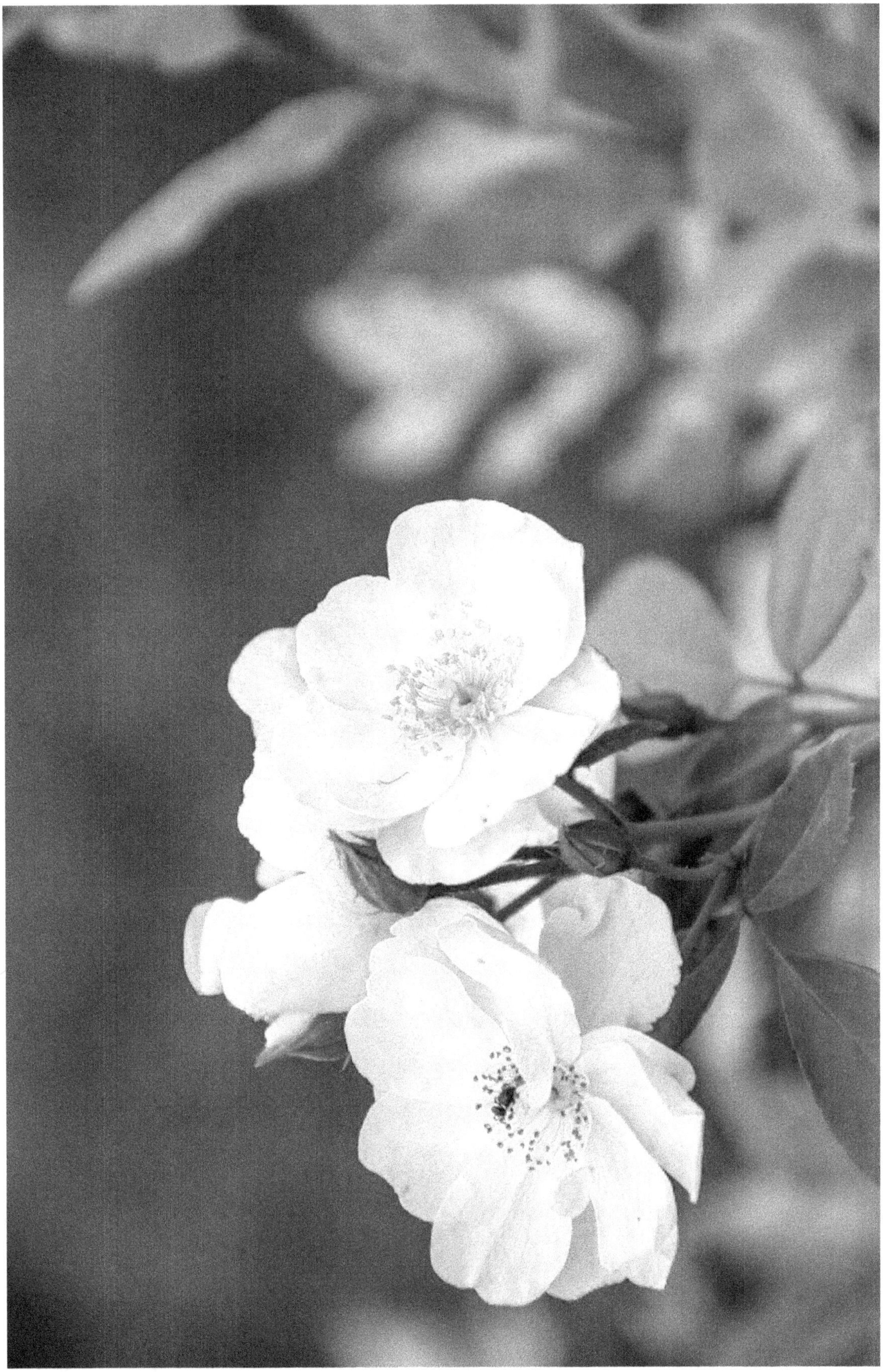

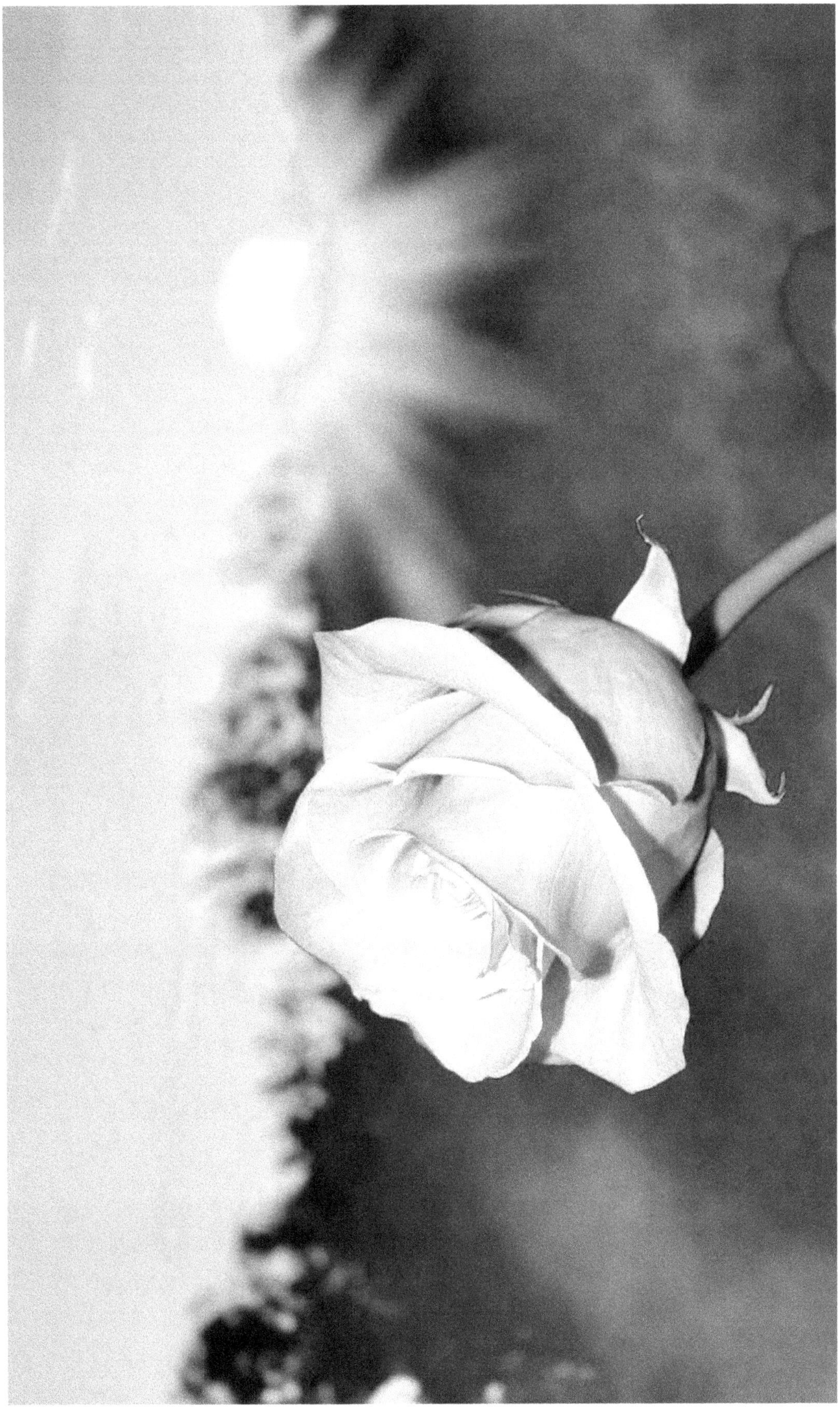

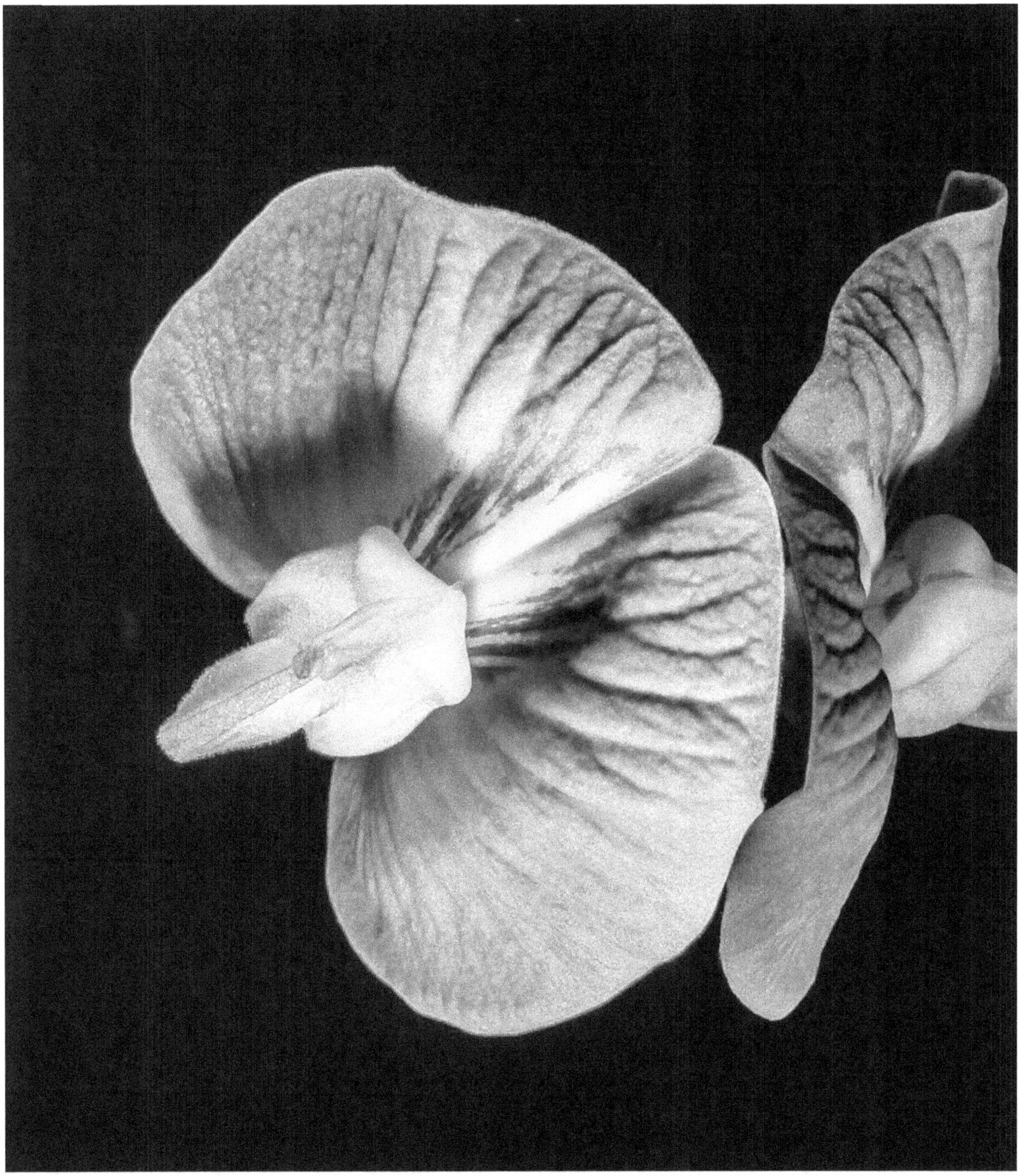

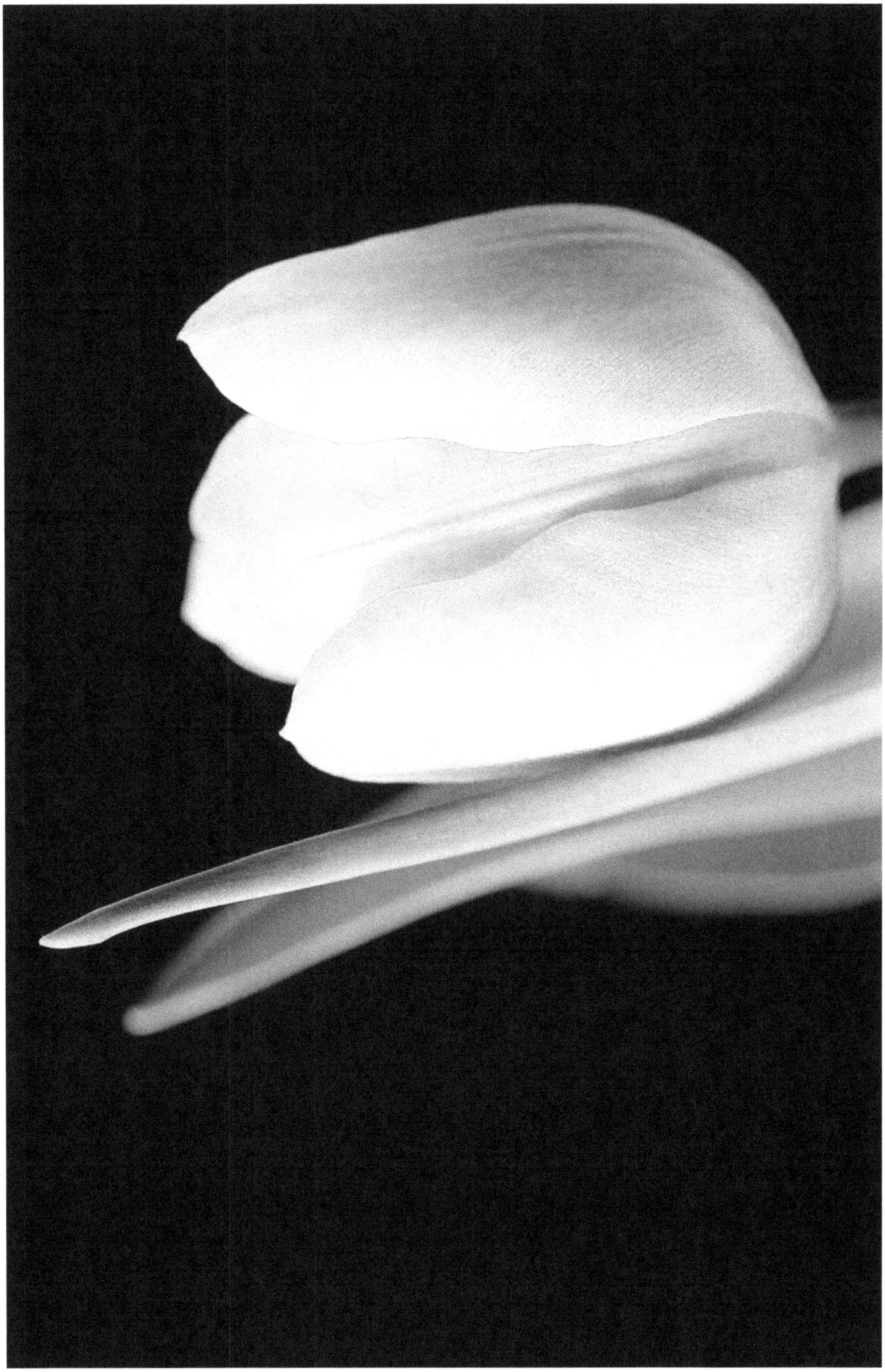

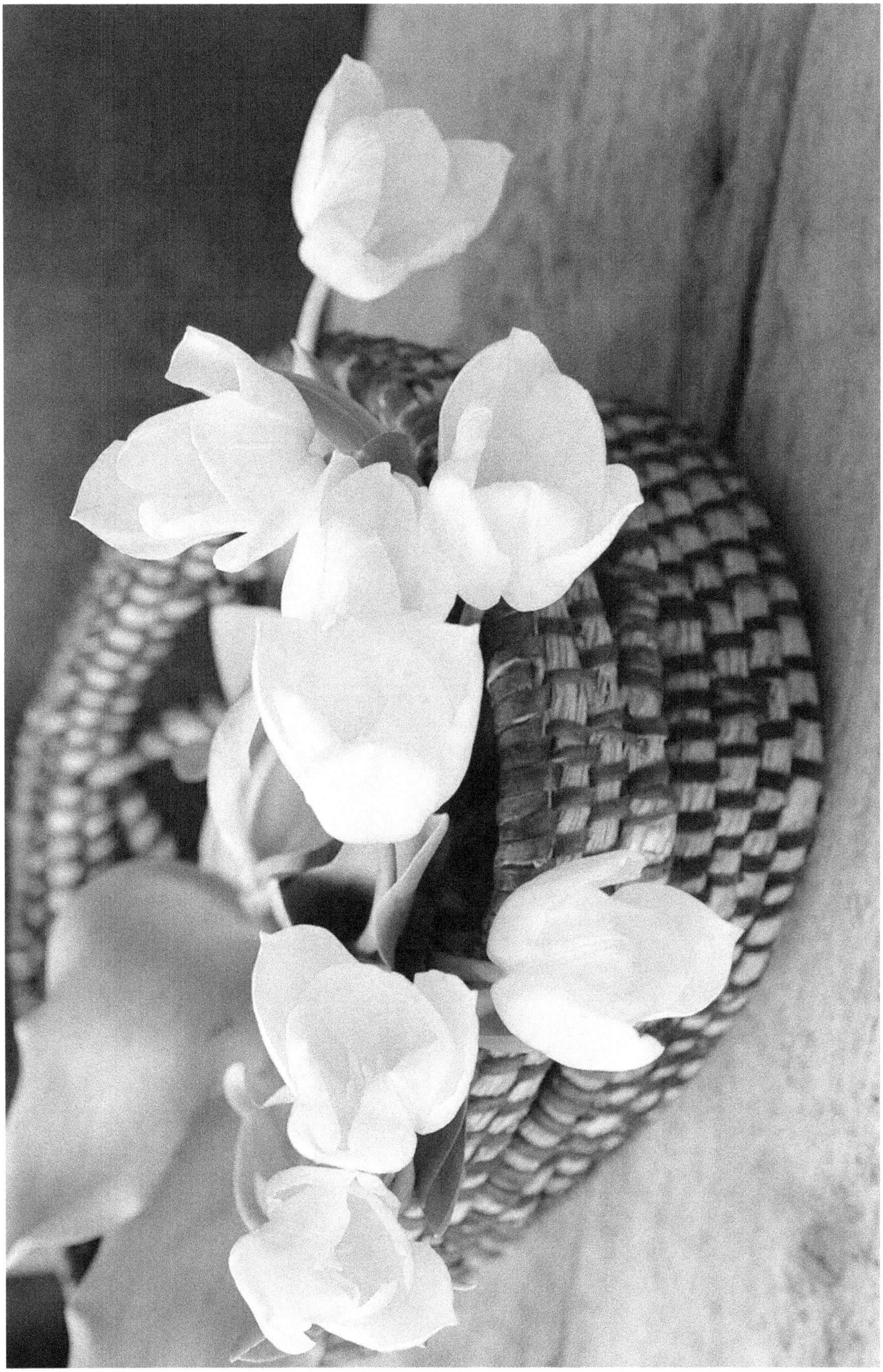

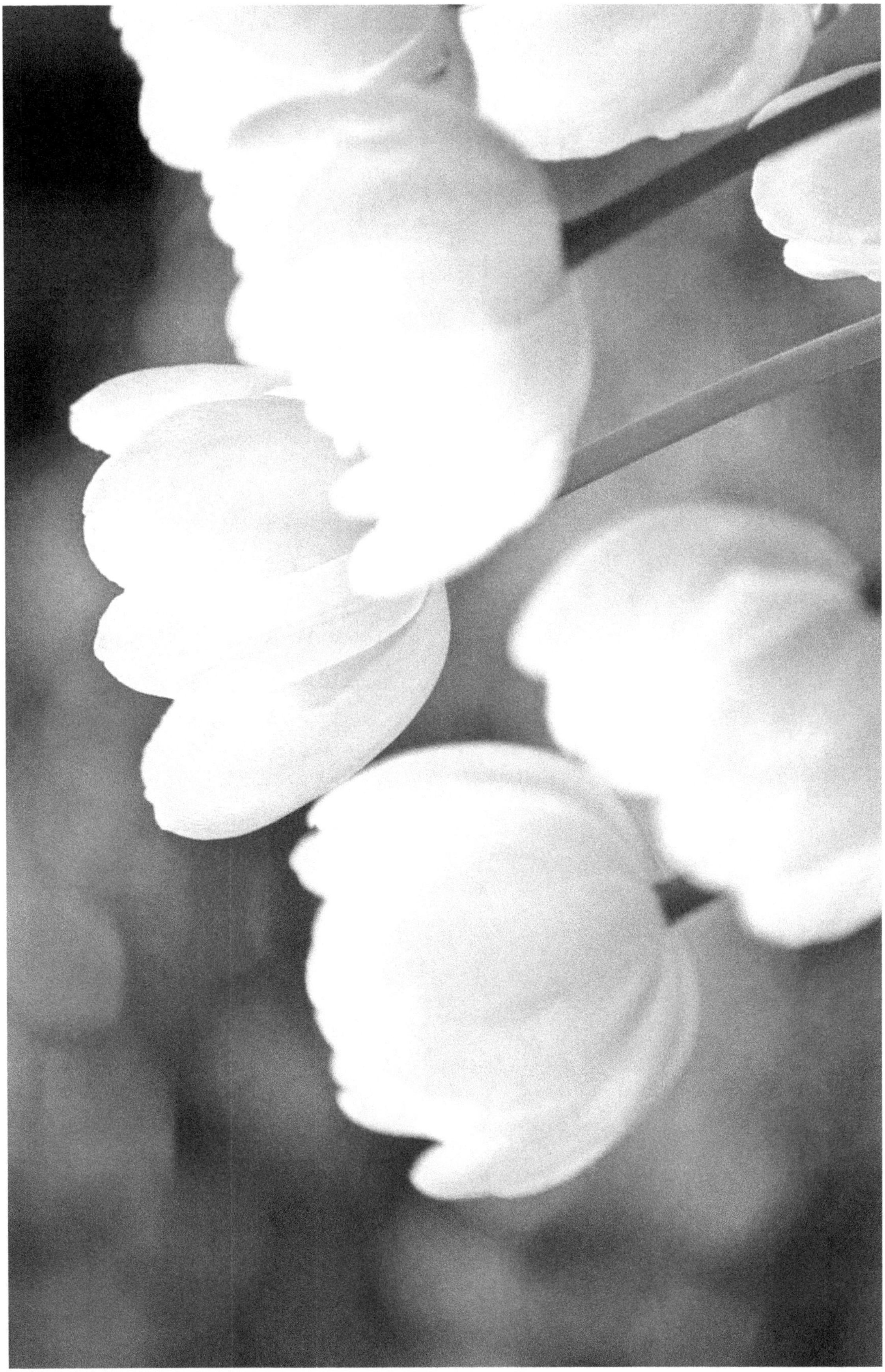

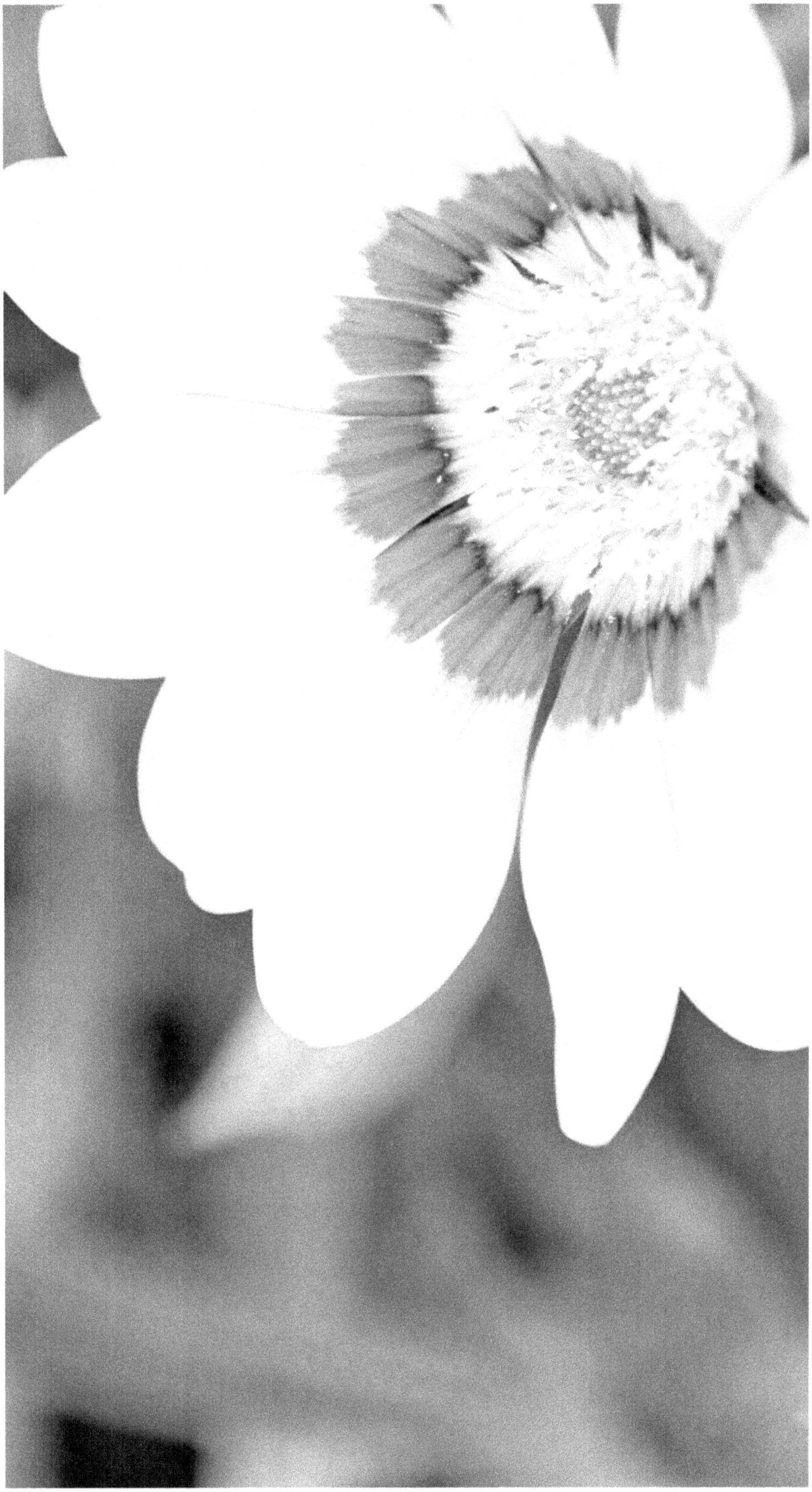

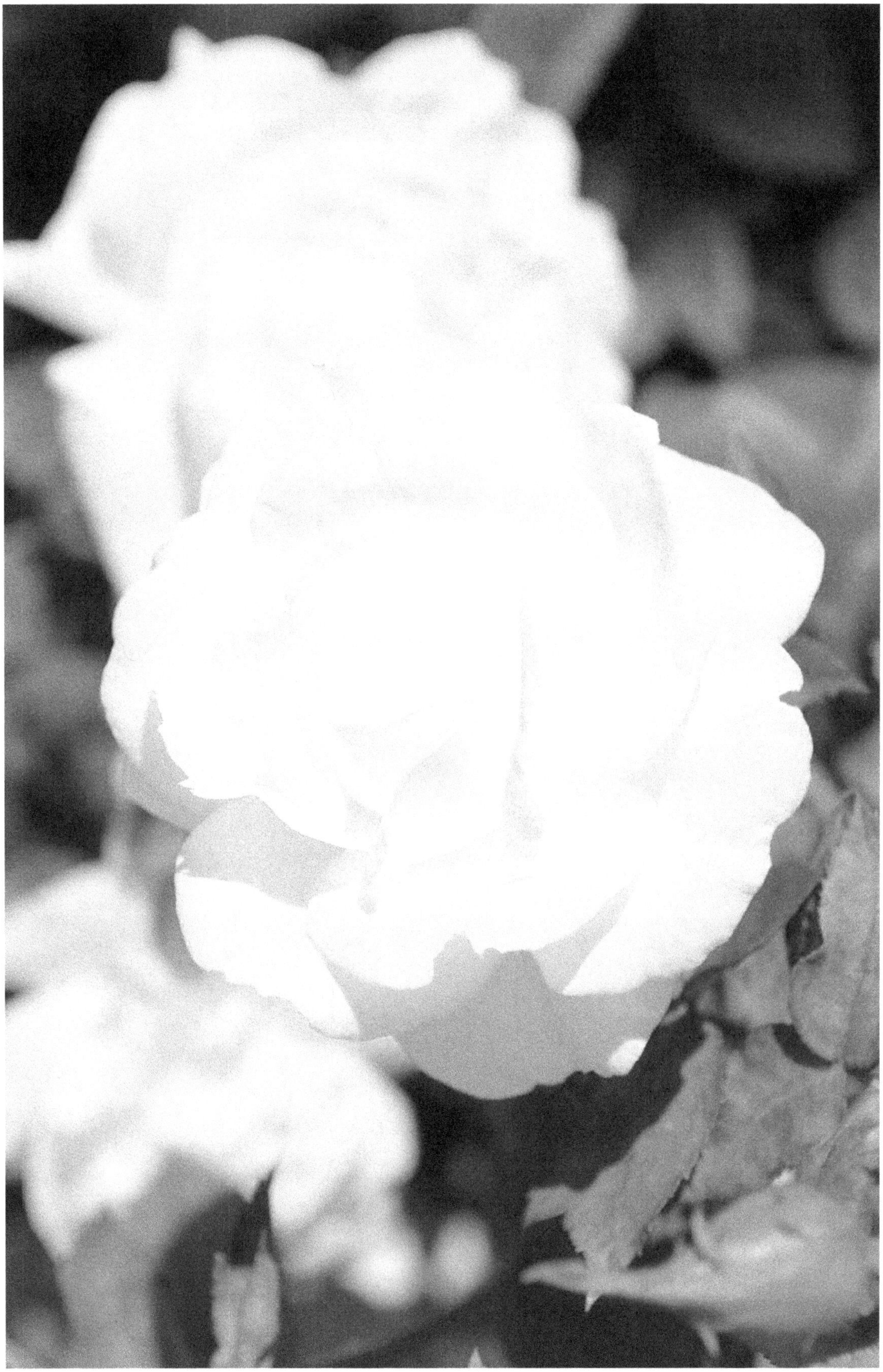

www.ingramcontent.com/pod-product-compliance
Lightning Source LLC
Chambersburg PA
CBHW081120280526
45787CB00007B/2910
* 9 7 8 1 5 3 5 0 6 8 7 7 2 *